THE VAGAL RESET

THE HIDDEN KEY TO RECLAIM YOUR ENERGY, COMBAT STRESS, AND EMBODY RESILIENCE

By

HELEN FOX

COPYRIGHT © 2024 HELEN FOX

LIMITS OF LIABILITY

AND DISCLAIMER OF WARRANTY

TABLE OF CONTENTS

READY TO RESET?

GRAB A CUPPA AND READ ON!

INTRODUCTION

There is never a doubt that stress has become a common part of life in today's fast-paced world, and it can have many adverse effects on our health. However, there's a remarkable tool within us called the vagus nerve that offers a pathway to self-regulation and healing. This nerve is a significant part of the parasympathetic nervous system and is responsible for triggering our relaxation response. This response acts as a counterbalance to the fight-or-flight reaction triggered by stress. Hence, by strengthening and activating our vagal tone, we can pave the way for a more resilient, peaceful, and balanced state of being. You will learn the practical experience of the benefits of this practice, and that is why this book is important to anyone who i looking to enhance their lifestyle.

More than just a book, it's an invitation to delve into the depths of your physiology and psychology. Within these pages, you'll discover the wisdom within you and learn practices supporting your overall health and well-being. This journey offers practical exercises and science-backed insights to help you cultivate a harmonious relationship between your body and mind. And by integrating these practices into your life, you will unlock long-lasting health and energy. As you embark on this journey, each chapter will build upon the last, guiding you toward a stress-free, energized, and optimally healthy existence. Whether your goal is to improve your physical health, enhance mental clarity, or cultivate emotional resilience, this book provides a comprehensive roadmap for achieving balance and vitality.

So, let's begin this adventure together. Step confidently into a life where health and vitality are not just aspirations but daily realities. Open your heart and mind to the endless possibilities that lie ahead on the vagal reset lifestyle—a path to a more vibrant, resilient, and fulfilled version of yourself. Welcome to a life where you are truly alive, strong, and content.

CHAPTER ONE

UNDERSTANDING THE VAGUS NERVE AND CORTISOL REGULATION

AMONG THE CRANIAL NERVES LINKING THE brain to the body, the vagus nerve stands out as a crucial element in our bodily and cognitive functions. Without it, even daily tasks would become challenging, yet its stimulation offers severe health benefits. Understanding the roles of the vagus nerves and how to enhance their function helps us make impactful changes that will be of great benefit to our health. While earthly treasures like gold and gems have always captured the interest of humans, the desire to understand all aspects of the human body represents a different kind of allure. Among the mysteries of human biology, the vagus nerve stands out as one that has attracted scholars due to its vital functions and unknown origins. This raises some intriguing questions, such as; what is the vagus nerve, and how did it come to play such an important function in our physiological framework?

Exploring the Anatomy and Function of the Vagus Nerve

The name "vagus nerve" comes from the Latin word vagus, which means "vagrant, wanderer," and refers to both the length and number of branches of this nerve. This vagus nerve, also called the vagal nerves, plays an important role in your body's parasympathetic nervous system, which oversees essential functions like digestion, heart rate, and immunity. These functions operate involuntarily, meaning you can't control them consciously.

The vagus nerves are the longest cranial nerves, extending from the brain to the large intestine. Emerging from your medulla oblongata, located in the lower part of your brainstem, these nerves traverse through various regions of your body, including:

Neck: They pass between your carotid artery and jugular vein.

Chest (Thorax): They make connections within your chest cavity.

Heart: The vagus nerves interact with your heart, influencing its activity.

Lungs: They extend into your lungs, contributing to respiratory function.

Abdomen and Digestive Tract: These nerves reach down into your abdomen and play a crucial role in regulating digestion and other gastrointestinal processes.

Before Stephen Porges presented the polyvagal theory, it was thought that the vagus nerve operated as a single neuronal circuit. However, the vagus nerve helps to maintain homeostasis by facilitating the regulation of numerous physiological processes. While the sympathetic chain, which comes from the spinal nerves, supports the condition of stress and mobilization for survival.

Main Functions of the Vagus Nerve

It regulates the heart: the vagus nerve helps the heart carry out its function by regulating the heart rate in slowing down the electrical impulses generated by the sinoatrial (SA) node, which serves as the heart's natural pacemaker. By modulating heart rate, the vagus nerve helps maintain proper cardiovascular function and contributes to heart rate variability.

1. **Parasympathetic Control:** it is primarily responsible for the parasympathetic control of many organs and structures in the body. It helps regulate activities that occur during rest, relaxation, and digestion. Stimulation of the vagus nerve tends to promote a "rest and digest" response, which includes slowing down the heart rate, lowering blood pressure, and increasing digestive processes.

2. **It Influences the Respiratory System:** It helps regulate breathing by controlling the smooth muscles in the bronchi and bronchioles of the lungs. Stimulation of the vagus nerve can lead to bronchoconstriction (narrowing of the airways) and a decrease in respiration rate.

3. **It Regulates the Gastrointestinal Functions:** The vagus nerve plays a significant role in the regulation of various gastrointestinal functions. It stimulates several organs, including the oesophagus, stomach, liver, pancreas, and intestines. It stimulates digestive enzyme secretion, promotes the contraction of smooth muscles in the gastrointestinal tract, and increases gastrointestinal blood flow, facilitating digestion and absorption of nutrients.

4. **It Controls the Sensory and Motor Functions:** The vagus nerve carries sensory information from organs in the thorax and abdomen back to the brain, providing afferent sensory input. It also controls certain motor functions, including movement of the muscles of the soft palate, pharynx, and larynx, contributing to speech, swallowing, and vocalization.

5. **It Modulates Inflammation**: The vagus nerve has anti-inflammatory effects and plays a role in regulating the immune response. It can inhibit the release of pro-inflammatory molecules, such as cytokines, and help maintain immune homeostasis.

The Role of the Parasympathetic Nervous System

Your parasympathetic nervous system regulates "rest and digest" functions, which are the opposite of the "fight or flight" response triggered by the sympathetic nervous system. Together, these two systems form your autonomic nervous system, which oversees involuntary bodily activities. When our vagus nerve is weak or has poor tone, we spend less time in the "rest and digest" mode and an immense amount of time in the "fight or flight" mode. This shift can lead to increased heart rate, blood pressure, and decreased digestion. Many people may notice that their anxiety or stress coincides with symptoms like acid reflux, which is linked to impaired digestion during periods of stress or sympathetic arousal. To support better digestion and overall health, I always advise my people to avoid "fight-or-flight dining." This means eating meals in a calm, non-stressful environment where they can chew thoroughly and take their time. Eating in the car or in front of the TV, especially when stressful or alarming news is on, can hinder digestion and contribute to feelings of anxiety.

However, being in a "fight or flight" state also affects our stress hormones, such as cortisol. Cortisol naturally rises in the morning to provide energy for the day, but some individuals may experience an elevated Cortisol Awakening Response (CAR), which can impact overall health. An elevated CAR is linked to insulin resistance, anxiety, brain fog, and inflammation. Additionally, cortisol levels may remain elevated throughout the day instead of tapering off as they should, which can occur in response to physical or emotional stress. One effective way to encourage relaxation and activate our body's "rest and digest" mode is by stimulating or strengthening the vagus nerve. A strong vagus nerve can play an important role in regulating mood, digestion, anxiety reduction, promoting relaxation, improving sleep quality, and even reducing inflammation and sugar cravings. The exciting part is that you can utilize several free and straightforward methods to enhance your vagus nerve tone from the comfort of your home with minimal effort. These methods will be explored in detail in the upcoming sections of this book. However, before diving into that, let's briefly examine the role of cortisol in the stress response.

Understanding the Role of Cortisol in the Stress Response

Cortisol is frequently referred to as the "stress hormone" due to its significant impact on the body's reaction to stress. It helps the body react to a perceived threat, raises blood sugar, and releases stored energy. It is also known as the "fight or flight" reaction. Cortisol is essential for several biological processes such as:

1. **Metabolism:** By controlling glucose levels, cortisol affects metabolism. It promotes the production of glucose by the body from non-carbohydrate sources, like amino acids, a process known as gluconeogenesis. This gives you energy when you're under stress.

2. **Immunological system:** Prolonged rise of cortisol may impair the immunological response and increase susceptibility to infections, but short-term surges in cortisol might temporarily suppress the immune system to refocus resources on more pressing demands.

3. **Anti-inflammatory:** The anti-inflammatory qualities of cortisol aid in the regulation and mitigation of inflammation inside the body. While this is advantageous in the short run, it may become troublesome if cortisol levels stay high for a long time.

4. **Blood Pressure:** By controlling the body's salt and water balance, cortisol affects blood pressure. High blood pressure can be attributed to elevated cortisol levels.

5. **Cycle of Sleep and Wakefulness:** Cortisol levels are greater in the early morning and decrease in the evening, according to the diurnal cycle. For the sleep-wake cycle to be regulated, this rhythm is essential.

6. **Mood States and Mental Processes**: Cortisol has an impact on both mood and mental clarity. Extended periods of elevated levels have been linked to mood problems and cognitive deficiencies. Though cortisol is necessary for many physiological functions, long-term increased amounts or chronic imbalances can cause health problems. Cortisol levels can be controlled in part by achieving a healthy lifestyle, minimizing stress, and obtaining enough sleep.

Examining the Connection between Vagal Tone, Cortisol Levels, and Energy Regulation

There is an intricate interplay that affects the body's response to vagal tone, cortisol levels, and energy regulation. The vagal tone is connected with better regulation of energy balance and metabolism. It influences the release of digestive enzymes and the function of insulin, which helps in the efficient use of energy from food. Furthermore, it can also promote calmness and relaxation, which may aid the reduction of overeating related to stress. Cortisol levels, especially when chronic, can disrupt normal energy regulation, leading to increased appetite, cravings for high-calorie foods, and accumulation of abdominal fat.

There is an interpersonal relationship between vagal tone and cortisol levels. A high vagal tone can help modulate the body's stress response, potentially leading to lower cortisol levels or a more regulated release of cortisol in response to stress. Conversely, chronic stress and high cortisol levels can negatively affect vagal tone, leading to reduced parasympathetic activity and a heightened stress response. Therefore, a healthy vagal tone can help manage stress and maintain balanced cortisol levels, which in turn supports proper energy regulation and overall metabolic health.

Conversely, chronic stress and disrupted cortisol patterns can negatively impact vagal tone and energy balance, potentially leading to health issues.

CHAPTER TWO

THE SCIENCE OF SOMATIC THERAPY

THE BASIC SCIENTIFIC PRINCIPLE OF SOMATIC therapy is neuroplasticity, which refers to the brain's ability to rearrange itself by generating new neural connections. This ability enables the brain to recover from traumas, diseases, and psychological problems like PTSD. Somatic therapy uses techniques such as deep breathing, relaxation exercises, and mild physical motions to help the body lessen the physiological symptoms of stress and trauma. It tries to restructure the neurological circuits connected with traumatic memories so that they no longer cause physical responses such as anxiety and fear. This treatment technique is also based on the polyvagal theory, which holds that the vagus nerve controls the heart rate, respiration, and digestive processes and can be manipulated to generate a state of relaxation. Somatic treatment techniques can stimulate the vagus nerve, which promotes relaxation and reduces trauma symptoms.

Introducing the Principles and Techniques of Somatic Therapy

Somatic psychology serves as the foundation for somatic therapy, a body-focused branch of psychology. It is accomplished by addressing a feedback loop that the body and mind are always in. In contrast to talk therapy, often known as psychotherapy, which is a popular form of treatment that is well-known, somatic therapy places a stronger emphasis on the body as the primary site of recovery. Practitioners of somatic therapy hold the belief that our bodies have the ability to hold on to our painful experiences. Back or neck discomfort, post-traumatic stress disorder, and other psychological disorders may result from these events if they are not dealt with in a timely manner (PTSD). Because of this, somatic therapists employ mind-body methods to help you relax and feel better both physically and emotionally.

Somatic therapists employ mind-body methods to help you let go of the stress that is negatively impacting your physical and mental health. There are different somatic techniques that are tailored to an individual's needs. These methods seek to encourage mental healing and foster a stronger feeling of body-mind connection in addition to relieving physical stress and discomfort.

Techniques Used During Somatic Therapy

Exercises for Body Awareness: The purpose of this technique is to increase the person's consciousness of their own body's positions, motions, and sensations in order to assist them become more sensitive to the physical expressions of their emotional moods. Techniques include mindful movement exercises like yoga or tai chi, guided meditations that concentrate on body sensations, and physical.

1. **Grounding Methods:** The goal is to calm anxiety and dissociation by assisting people to be present in the moment and connected to their surroundings. Techniques are deep diaphragmatic breathing, walking

barefoot, and mindfulness exercises that concentrate on the senses (such as sounds, sights, or tactile sensations).

2. **Breathwork:** The goal of breathwork is to lessen tension, encourage relaxation and emotional discharge, and control the autonomic nervous system. Techniques are breathing exercises that are controlled, such as breath pacing, deep abdominal breathing, and alternate nostril breathing.

3. **Exercises for Movement:** The goal is to enhance mobility, reduce physical stress, and allow the body to communicate emotions. Techniques yoga, dance, stretches, and other gentle, mindful activities that promote the investigation of bodily motions and the emotions associated with them.

4. **Pandiculation**: By voluntarily contracting and relaxing muscles, this process relieves tension and resets muscle length. Techniques such as a yawn or stretch upon waking include consciously tensing the muscles, slowly stretching, and then gently releasing the tension.

Exploring How Somatic Exercises Affect the Nervous System

There are several ways that somatic exercises might affect the nervous system. They are:

1. **Motion and Learning:** Our neurological system contains a region known as the basal ganglia. This region is important for somatic movement

because it is linked to voluntary or conscious motor actions, the acquisition of procedural skills, habit development, eye movements, and the general process of learning and understanding via cognition, experiences, and senses. Emotion is also important in this context. The thalamus transmits output from the basal ganglia, which it gets from the cortex, back to the motor regions of the cortex. The basal ganglia aid in the body's ability to initiate and stop motions. We can control muscle tone and suppress undesired motions in this region.

2. **Memory**: The Cingulate Gyrus is one of your Limbic System's main structures. This area supports the control of mood. It also determines our reaction to external stimuli. It is essential for giving us the ability to choose our course of action and respond appropriately to things and situations outside of ourselves.

3. **Sensory Organ:** The cingulate gyrus, located in front of the thalamus, is crucial to the effectiveness of somatic therapy. This area is made up of grey matter that helps process sensory information. It is the ultimate receiver of impulses from the tongue, hearing, eyes, and skin sensors. After receiving these impulses, the thalamus distributes them to various areas of the cerebral cortex, promoting sensory integration, which is critical in somatic therapy.

Understanding the Mind-Body Connection and its Impact on Stress and Energy Levels

The system by which the body and mind interact allows for the influence of one on the other's physical and mental states. Our emotions: happy, sad, or stressed affect our general health and sense of wellbeing. Our body's reaction to stress is mediated by the sympathetic nervous system and the hypothalamic-pituitary-adrenal (HPA) axis. If psychological stress is not adequately controlled, it can cause the body to release cortisol, which can impact multiple physical functions and eventually lead to chronic stress.

When there are high cortisol levels, it can cause abnormalities in metabolism, sleep cycles, and energy levels. These effects can cause symptoms of exhaustion and low vitality. The vagus nerve, an essential part of the parasympathetic nervous system, influences mood, digestion, and heart rate. It also plays a major role in the mind-body link. Better mood control, stress resilience, and general energy levels are linked to high vagal tones.

CHAPTER THREE

UNVEILING THE POWER OF BREATHWORK

HAVE YOU EVER EXPERIENCED ANXIETY OR tension, and the moment you take a deep, slow breath, you are relaxed? That is because deep breathing promotes relaxation. It's an excellent weapon in the battle against stress. Breathing deeply and slowly has numerous health advantages and therapeutic uses. It is an essential component of many contemplative traditions as a result. Martial arts, yoga, and meditation all involve deliberate, slow breathing techniques.

Exploring the Relationship between Breathing Patterns and Vagal Tone

Breathing patterns have a significant impact on vagal tone, making it an effective method to improve health and reduce stress. Here's how to do it:

1. **Breathe Slowly and Deeply:** Breathing slowly and deeply increases vagal tone by stimulating the parasympathetic nervous system via the vagus nerve. This breathing technique lowers the heart rate and encourages calm. Focusing on lengthening exhalations in comparison to inhalations, which promotes the body's relaxation response, is the standard advice for improving vagal tone.

2. **The Frequency of Resonance Breathing:** This is a particular breathing technique wherein you breathe at your own resonance frequency, which is typically between 5.5 and 6 breaths per minute for most adults. Resonance frequency breathing is much slower than most adults' typical respiratory rate of 12 to 18 breaths per minute. Studies show that

breathing at this frequency optimizes heart rate variability (HRV), which is a vagal tone-related measure of the variance in time between each heartbeat. Improved emotional control, stress resilience, and cardiovascular health are all linked to higher HRV.

3. **Yoga and Pranayama:** Yoga exercises, particularly pranayama (breath control techniques), might improve vagal tone. The relaxing benefits of some techniques on the neurological system, such as Ujjayi (ocean breath), Bhramari (bee breath), and Nadi Shodhana (alternate nostril breathing), are particularly noteworthy. These breathing techniques not only improve mindfulness and relaxation, but they also play an important role in controlling the body's physiological responses via vagal tone. Improved vagal tone can lead to better digestion, a lower heart rate, and less stress, all of which promote general well-being. Here are the guidelines for using them and their impacts on the vagal tone:

4. **Ujjayi Breath (Ocean Breath): It** travels down the neck alongside the carotid arteries. The slight resistance caused by throat compression can convey relaxing signals to the vagus nerve, increasing parasympathetic (relaxation) activity and boosting vagal tone.

   a. **How to:** Sit comfortably, with your spine straight. Start by inhaling deeply through your nose. As you exhale, slightly restrict the back of your throat and produce a faint hissing sound like that of the water. Continue to breathe deeply, with the throat constricted on both the inhale and exhale. This should result in a constant ocean-like sound.

5. **Bhramari Breath (Bee Breath)**: The humming sound of Bhramari breath activates the   vagus nerve, which has a calming impact on the brain and raises vagal tone. This leads to increased stress resilience and a lower inflammatory response.

   a. **How To:** Sit in a peaceful, pleasant area. Close your eyes and relax your face. Put your index fingers on the cartilage of your ears. Take a deep breath in and exhale, softly pressing your fingers into the cartilage while humming like a bee. Repeat multiple times, concentrating on the music to clear your thoughts.

6. **Nadi Shodhana (Alternate Nostril Breathing):** It helps to balance the autonomic nervous system by alternating between sympathetic (fight or flight) and parasympathetic (rest and digest) responses. Regular practice helps to control vagal tone by encouraging relaxation and lowering physiological stress markers.

   a. **How To**: Sit comfortably with an upright spine. Place your left hand on your knee and your right thumb against your right nose. Close the right nostril and breathe in slowly through the left. Close the left nostril with your ring finger, then open the right nostril and slowly exhale through it. Inhale through the right nostril, then close it. Open the left nostril and exhale through it.

This completes a single cycle. Continue for many rounds, switching the nostrils through which you inhale and exhale.

To get the most out of the benefits of vagal tone, it is advisable that you perfect your breathing technique when starting out. Mastering the skills enables proper application and provides a safe environment for exploring the physical and psychological impacts of breathwork.

Introducing Various Breathwork Techniques for Stress Reduction and Relaxation

These techniques are simple to implement into everyday schedules to help lower stress levels, strengthen mental health, and improve general health. The following are a few breathwork methods for relaxation and stress relief, along with guidelines for using them:

1. **Belly Breathing, Or Diaphragmatic Breathing:** This basic method can lower heart rate and promote muscular relaxation while promoting complete oxygen exchange.

    a. **How to:** Take a comfortable seat or lie down, and place one hand on your stomach and the other on your chest. Breathe in deeply via your nose, making sure your chest stays mostly motionless and your tummy expands against your hand. Using your pursed lips, gently release the air while contracting your abdominal muscles. Practice for ten minutes every day, aiming to achieve six to ten slow, deep breaths per minute.

2. **Breathing in 4-7-8:** The 4-7-8 approach, created by Dr. Andrew Weil, is a straightforward but effective strategy that encourages serenity and relaxation.

   a. **How to:** Start by fully exhaling through your mouth. As you count to four, silently inhale through your nose with closed lips. For seven counts, hold your breath. Next, release all of the air via your mouth while producing an eight-count whoosh sound. Cycles can be repeated up to four times.

3. **Square breathing or box breathing:** Navy SEALs employ this approach to increase focus and relax the nervous system.

   a. **How to do it:** Breathe in for four counts, hold it in for four counts, release it for four counts, and then hold it for another four counts. Continue doing this for a few minutes. It is especially useful in high-stress scenarios.

4. **Contrary Nostril Inhalation (Nadi Shodhana):** This yoga pose is often performed with the intention of calming the mind and balancing the body.

   a. **How to:** Take a seat comfortably. Close one nostril by pressing the thumb of one hand against it. Using your fingers, seal the other nostril after taking a slow breath. Breathe out slowly via your open first nostril. Continue doing this, switching nostrils with each breath. Count on five to ten cycles.

5. **Frequency of Inhaling:** This is breathing at your own frequency, which is usually between 5.5 and 6 breaths per minute. It's said to improve heart rate variability.

    a. **How to:** Look for a peaceful spot to lay down or sit. Set a timer and start inhaling for five counts and exhaling for five counts. Find a rhythm that is comfortable and permits strain-free deep, relaxing breaths by adjusting the timing as necessary.

Tips for Exercise

1. **The Secret Is Consistency**: The effectiveness of these approaches for relaxation and stress reduction grows with regular use.
2. **Pleasant Environment:** Select a comfy, peaceful area where you won't be bothered. To maximize the benefits of mindfulness, try focusing only on your breathing and the here and now.
3. **As necessary, adjust:** You are welcome to modify the numbers and approaches to suit your needs. Not perfection, but relaxation and a reduction in stress is the aim.

By incorporating these breathwork methods into your daily schedule, you can build an effective toolset for stress relief and improved relaxation. Never forget that it's a good idea to speak with a healthcare professional before beginning any new wellness regimen, particularly if you have any underlying medical issues.

Understanding the Physiological Effects of Breathwork on Cortisol Regulation and Energy Levels

Imagine your body as a bustling city at rush hour, with cortisol representing the traffic that congests the roads, producing stress and delays across the cityscape. Breathwork is therefore related to an excellently timed traffic signal system, which regulates vehicle flow to ensure smooth transit and reduces traffic congestion. When you practice breathwork, it's as if you're turning on a succession of green lights, calming the rush, relieving cortisol traffic, and enabling energy to flow freely, similar to clear, open roads. This not only reduces stress in the city (your body), but also increases energy and efficiency, making it a more pleasant and productive place to live.

The main functions of breathing are the actions of the lungs to take in oxygen and release carbon dioxide. The diaphragm, a strip of muscle beneath the lungs, and the muscles in between the ribs are the muscles that regulate lung movement. A person's breathing pattern alters while they are under stress. Anxious people usually breathe in tiny, shallow breaths, pushing air into and out of their lungs with their shoulders rather than their diaphragm. The body's gas equilibrium is upset by this breathing pattern. Hyperventilation, or shallow over breathing, can exacerbate the physical signs of stress and hence prolong worry. Breathing exercises can help alleviate some of these symptoms. A relaxed person breathes slowly, evenly, and gently via their nostrils. Replicating a peaceful breathing pattern on purpose appears to soothe the neurological system that governs the body's automatic processes. Controlled breathing can result in physiological changes such as decreased heart rate and blood pressure, less stress hormones in the blood, less lactic acid accumulation in muscle tissue, balanced blood levels of carbon dioxide and oxygen, and enhanced immune system performance.

CHAPTER FOUR

CULTIVATING MINDFULNESS AND PRESENCE

T O UNDERSTAND THE FUNCTION OF MINDFULNESS in controlling vagal tone, you must examine the intricate relationship that exists between the neurological system, the mind, and general bodily health. The vagus nerve is a vital part of the parasympathetic nervous system that regulates many important body processes like heart rhythm, digestion, and immunological response, is indicated by vagal tone. While a low vagal tone is linked to poor health outcomes, a high vagal tone is linked to improved physical and mental well-being.

Understanding the Role of Mindfulness in Vagal Tone Regulation

Practices that promote focused awareness and relaxation, such as mindfulness, have a major impact on vagal tone. Here is a closer look at how mindfulness affects vagal tone modulation:

1. By stimulating the parasympathetic nervous system, these techniques aid in calming the body and lowering stress levels. Vagus nerve stimulation is directly linked to this activation, which may raise vagal tone.

2. Mindfulness gives people the ability to better control their negative emotions by raising their awareness of their own emotional states. Vagal tone and the vagus nerve's ability to function are directly related to this modulation of emotion.

3. Mindfulness techniques help the body respond less to stress by activating the parasympathetic nervous system more and the sympathetic nervous system less (also known as the "fight or flight" reaction).

The relationship between enhanced vagal tone and mindfulness has been substantiated by numerous studies. Studies have demonstrated that practicing mindfulness can raise heart rate variability (HRV), which is an indicator of improved vagal tone. The increase in vagal tone was suggested by a study that was published in the "Journal of Alternative and complem- - entary Medicine" and found that participants in an 8-week program of mindfulness-based stress reduction (MBSR) showed increased HRV. A useful and approachable strategy for people who want to improve their vagal tone is to incorporate mindfulness practices into their everyday routine since it suggests that mindfulness techniques might help manage stress, enhance mental health, and promote physical well-being in general.

In addition, by encouraging relaxation, enhancing emotional regulation, and lowering the stress response in the body, mindfulness plays a critical role in controlling vagal tone. Regular mindfulness practice can improve both physical and mental health outcomes by supporting the autonomic nervous system's natural equilibrium.

Introducing Mindfulness Practices to Enhance Body Awareness and Presence.

By incorporating mindfulness exercises into your everyday routine, you can reap several mental and physical health advantages by becoming more present and aware of your body. Being mindful entails being open, curious, and judgment-free when observing the current moment. The following mindfulness exercises are especially meant to improve bodily awareness and presence:

1. **Mindful Breathing:** One of the core mindfulness exercises is mindful breathing, which includes paying attention to your breath. You don't try to alter the rhythm of your inhalations and exhalation;

    a. you just watch how they naturally occur. This exercise is a flexible way to improve body awareness and mindfulness because it may be done anywhere, at any time.

2. **Body Scan Meditation:** During Body Scan Meditation, you mentally "scan" your entire body from head to toe while lying down and recording any pain, stress, or other sensations. Your awareness of your body's demands and the places that need rest or attention will increase as a result of this practice.

3. **Mindful Movement techniques:** Such as yoga, tai chi, and qigong, entails moving mindfully and paying attention to your body's sensations. These exercises cultivate a sense of conscious presence, increase body awareness, and strengthen muscles and ligaments.

4. **Mindful Eating:** The mindful eating technique entails giving your entire attention to the eating and drinking experience, both inside and out. You take note of your meal's hues, fragrances, tastes, textures, and sensations of fullness and hunger. Eating with awareness can turn a mundane action into a really fulfilling and joyful one.

5. **Outdoor Walks:** Going for walks in the outdoors while paying attention to the sights, sounds, and smells around you can help you establish a strong connection with the natural world and help you stay grounded in the present.

6. **Paying Attention:** Concentrating attention on a single sense at a time, including paying close attention to noises or seeing the colors and shapes around you, you can lessen the influence of distracting ideas and increase your awareness of the current moment by doing this.

7. **Loving-kindness Meditation:** This increases body awareness by fostering an attentive and compassionate relationship with one's own body, even if its main goal is to cultivate pleasant sentiments toward oneself and others.

Including these mindfulness exercises into your daily routine can help you become more aware of your body, manage your stress, better control your emotions, and feel better overall. You might experience a stronger sense of connectedness to both the outside world and yourself as you grow more aware of the here and now and the sensations in your body.

Exploring how Mindfulness can Influence Cortisol Levels and Energy Regulation

Engaging in mindfulness techniques has a significant positive effect on physiological functions, such as energy balance and cortisol regulation in the body. The adrenal glands release cortisol, also known as the "stress hormone," in reaction to stress and low blood glucose levels. Chronically high cortisol levels can cause a number of health problems, such as chronic fatigue, anxiety, depression, and poor cognitive function, even though cortisol is essential for immune system function, energy regulation, and preserving homeostasis. There are various important ways that mindfulness techniques might enhance energy regulation and lower cortisol levels:

1. **Reduces stress:** It has been demonstrated that mindfulness meditation lowers perceived stress, which is a major factor in cortisol release. Mindfulness can reduce cortisol levels by fostering a state of calm awareness and accepting the current moment without passing judgment. This can lessen the body's natural stress response.

2. **Improved Sleep Quality**: Insomnia and poor sleep quality can raise cortisol levels, especially at night, upsetting the body's normal circadian pattern of cortisol release. Increased energy regulation during the day and regulated cortisol levels are both influenced by getting enough sleep.

3. **Improved emotional regulation:** By raising awareness of thoughts and feelings without triggering an instant reaction, mindfulness improves emotional regulation. The frequency and intensity of emotional stressors

that cause cortisol release may be decreased as a result of this enhanced regulation.

4. **Improved Energy:** Including yoga and mindful walking, can have a favorable impact on cortisol levels and energy balance. Regular exercise has been demonstrated to lower cortisol levels and enhance energy metabolism, resulting in a more efficient and well-balanced utilization of energy sources throughout the day.

5. **Science-Based Proof:** Numerous researches back up the positive effects of mindfulness on energy control and cortisol levels. For example, an 8-week Mindfulness-Based Stress Reduction (MBSR) program was found to significantly lower participants' cortisol levels (a study published in "Health Psychology" reported this effect). Another study published in "Psychoneuroendocrinology" found that people who trained in mindfulness meditation had lower cortisol responses to stress, which may indicate better energy regulation and stress resilience.

In conclusion, a promising strategy for controlling cortisol levels and improving energy regulation is to engage in mindfulness techniques. For those looking to enhance their energy regulation and stress management, mindfulness is still a useful tool as the scientific community investigates these advantages.

CHAPTER FIVE

THE ROLE OF MOVEMENT IN VAGAL TONE REGULATION

Including movement in daily life to control vagal tone benefits mental and physical health in equal measure. It lowers stress and improves cardiovascular resilience while also fostering emotional well-being through better social interaction and emotional management. The selection of an activity can be customized to meet the needs and interests of each individual, highlighting the necessity of consistent participation for the best results.

Exploring the Connection between Movement, Vagal Tone, and Cortisol Regulation

Movement, vagal tone, and cortisol control are linked in an intriguing trio that highlights the complex interplay in the body between the neurological system, hormone responses, and physical activity. Every component is essential to preserving health and wellbeing, and their interconnections provide insights into holistic strategies for stress management, resilience building, and the promotion of general physical and mental health.

Consistent physical activity, particularly mindfulness and breath-control techniques like tai chi and yoga, can improve vagal tone. Better emotional regulation and a more robust stress response are correlated with increased vagal tone via movement.

Physical activity affects the hypothalamic-pituitary-adrenal (HPA) axis, which regulates the release of cortisol. Regular, moderate physical activity helps restore normal cortisol rhythms, which lowers the likelihood of long-term stress and the health problems it brings.

A higher vagal tone is linked to a more balanced activation and recovery of the HPA axis, which results in more flexible cortisol reactions to stress. This implies that people with stronger vagal tones may recover to baseline levels more quickly and have less noticeable cortisol rises in response to stress.

Introducing Somatic Movement Exercises to Release Tension and Promote Relaxation

Exercises using somatic movement center on the inner sensation of movement as opposed to the result or appearance from the outside. These physical activities aim to improve your awareness of your body, soothe tense muscles, and encourage rest and recovery. People can affect their vagal tone and cortisol levels through somatic movement, which helps with stress reduction and emotional management. To relieve stress and promote relaxation, try incorporating any of these somatic movement techniques into your daily routine:

1. **Diaphragmatic Breathing:** This method of breathing expands the abdomen rather than the chest by encouraging the diaphragm to fully contract during inhalation. It causes vagus nerve stimulation, which can aid in lowering cortisol levels and raising vagal tone, thereby fostering calm.

2. **Position for Constructive Rest**: Pandiculation refers to the natural behavior of stretching and yawning. Stretching, similar to pandiculation, can benefit human health and well-being. When we stretch our muscles in this manner, we are effectively replicating the natural pandiculation process. This sort of stretching helps to reestablish muscle length and relieve chronic muscle tightness. Muscles that are consistently tight can shorten and become dysfunctional over time, resulting in discomfort and impaired functional capacity.

   a. **How to**: Lay flat on your back with your feet hip-width apart and your knees bent. You can rest your hands at your sides or place them on your abdomen. This posture promotes relaxation and eases tension by allowing the pelvic floor and back muscles to be gently released.

3. **The Feldenkrais Method:** This approach enhances general body awareness and improves movement patterns through deliberate attention and gentle movement. By pointing out tense spots and unconsciously patterned movement that add to stress, the Feldenkrais Method provides a technique to release them.

4. **Alexander Method**: Through this educational process, people can learn how to walk more naturally and with better posture throughout daily activities. It facilitates better breathing, alignment, and a reduction in tense muscles, all of which contribute to relaxation and stress relief.

5. **Tai Chi and Qigong:** These traditional Chinese forms of exercise incorporate breathing techniques, meditation, and slow, deliberate motions. Tai Chi and Qigong's soft, flowing motions can help lower cortisol levels, enhance vagal tone, and lessen stress.

6. **Dance Movement Therapy**: This type of movement therapy promotes using dance as a vehicle for emotional expression. It can be a potent method for reducing stress, elevating mood, and promoting wellbeing.

7. **Yoga:** There are some poses and sequences that are quite helpful for releasing tension in the muscles. For unwinding and lowering tension, restorative and Yin yoga forms are especially beneficial.

These exercises not only ease tense muscles but also positively affect vagal tone and cortisol levels, which in turn foster a feeling of peace and wellbeing. Through increasing their awareness of their own body's feelings, people can develop a more profound sense of calm and resilience to stress.

Understanding the Benefits of Integrating Movement into Daily Routines for Energy Renewal

Regular physical activity has many positive effects on mood, cognitive function, and general energy levels, in addition to its effects on physical health. Here's a closer look at how adding movement might boost energy:

1. **Improves Energy:** Regular exercise raises energy levels because it improves cardiovascular system efficiency, which increases the amount of oxygen and nutrients that can reach tissues and organs.

2. **Improves Sleep Quality:** Exercise facilitates sleep by assisting in the regulation of the body's circadian cycle. Improved sleep quality is essential for energy restoration since it promotes healing and rejuvenation of the body and mind.

3. **Reduces Anxiety and Stress**: Being active is a powerful way to reduce stress. It causes the body to produce more endorphins, which are naturally occurring mood enhancers that can lower stress, ease anxiety, and promote wellbeing.

4. **Improves Cognitive Ability and Mental Health:** Research has demonstrated that physical activity can improve mental health by mitigating feelings of anxiety and depression.

5. **Improves mitochondrial health**: The "powerhouses" of the cell that produce energy, the mitochondria, are stimulated to produce new ones during exercise. Physical activity can boost the body's capacity to create energy, resulting in increased stamina and general vitality via raising mitochondrial density.

CHAPTER SIX

NURTURING CONNECTION AND SOCIAL ENGAGEMENT

OUR EMOTIONAL HEALTH AND GENERAL well-being depend on social interaction and connection cultivation. Since we are social beings by nature, the relationships we have with other people have a major impact on our emotional state, degree of stress, and even physical health.

Exploring the Social Engagement System and its Impact on Vagal Tone

Vagal tone is directly influenced by the social engagement system, which is crucial for human stress response and emotional regulation. The muscles in the face and voice, which are necessary for facial expressions, vocalization, listening, and head movements, are controlled by the ventral vagal complex, which is linked to the social engagement system. This system's activation encourages social connection as well as tranquility and safety, both of which are essential for regulating emotions and reducing stress.

Positive social interactions have been shown to dramatically improve vagal tone, as seen by elevated heart rate variability (HRV). Good health is indicated by a high HRV, which also suggests a robust and adaptable stress response system. The social interaction system lowers cortisol levels, lessens the stress response, and encourages a feeling of calm and wellbeing when it is functioning.

Our capacity to create and preserve social ties, which are essential for emotional support and stress resilience, is influenced by our social engagement system. Increased vagal tone from fulfilling social interactions can result in improved emotional control, which in turn facilitates social engagement. This can set off a positive feedback loop.

How to Improve Social Engagement Framework

1. **Mindful Listening**: Paying attention and listening without passing judgment on what is being said can improve social interaction and strengthen bonds with people, which will have a beneficial effect on vagal tone.

2. **Face Exercises:** These exercises have the ability to increase vagal tone and improve emotional well-being by stimulating the ventral vagal complex. The jaw release exercise - is an excellent approach to strengthen the muscles around your chin and jawline. Sit or stand with a straight spine and relaxed shoulders. Gently flex your jaw as if you were chewing, but maintain your lips closed. Inhale deeply, and as you exhale, widen your mouth and thrust out your tongue. Hold this stance for a few seconds before releasing and repeating the technique several times.

3. **Chin Lifts:** This is a fantastic way to strengthen the muscles beneath your chin and achieve a more defined jawline. Stand up straight and tip your head back, looking at the ceiling. Pucker your lips as if you're attempting to kiss the ceiling. Hold this position for a few seconds, then release.

Repeat Chin Lifts several times to strengthen your chin and neck muscles.

4. **Kiss the Ceiling:** Kiss the Ceiling is a simple yet effective exercise for decreasing double chin. To do it, tilt your head back and imagine reaching out to kiss the ceiling. Hold this position for a few seconds to feel the stretch in your neck and chin muscles.

5. **Chanting and Singing:** Vocalization-based group activities, like chanting or singing, can turn on the social engagement system and provide a feeling of belonging.

6. **Laughing Yoga:** This type of yoga integrates the health advantages of yoga breathing with the power of laughing to enhance mood, vagal tone, and social interaction system.

7. **Eye Contact:** By keeping a gentle eye contact during a conversation, you can activate the social engagement system and foster feelings of trust and connection.

Engaging in practices that promote positive social interactions and stimulate the ventral vagal complex can lead to improvements in vagal tone, demonstrating the intricate link between our social world and physiological health.

Introducing Practices for Fostering Connection and Social Engagement

The following activities are intended to strengthen social ties and promote a feeling of community:

1. **Active Listening**: Try your best to listen intently to other people without preparing your answer in advance of their words. By nodding, keeping eye contact, and asking follow-up questions, you can demonstrate that you are paying attention.

2. **Express Gratitude**: Consistently show appreciation to others in your vicinity. This can be accomplished through words of gratitude, cards of appreciation, or tiny acts of kindness.

3. **Group physical activities**: Take part in hiking clubs, team sports, and dancing lessons. Exercise that is done together not only improves health but also strengthens social ties by promoting a sense of accomplishment and togetherness.

4. **Getting Involved in Interest-Based Clubs and Groups**: Participate in clubs or community groups to meet people who have similar interests. Whether it's a computer enthusiast group, a gardening community, or a reading club, common interests serve as a solid basis for meaningful social relationships.

5. **Volunteering**: You can meet like-minded people by lending your time and expertise to a cause that you support. Volunteering can result in the

formation of strong ties through shared beliefs and group activities, as well as a sense of purpose.

6. **Practice Mindfulness and Compassion**: Participating in activities that foster compassion and mindfulness, like meditation, can help you become more empathic and better able to relate to people.

7. Invest in Communication Skills Workshops: Attending workshops or classes on improving communication skills can greatly increase your capacity to establish and preserve social relationships.

8. **Attend Social Gatherings:** Create regular social events, such as family game evenings or weekly dinners with friends. Relationships can be strengthened, and a dependable source of social support can be offered by consistency.

9. **Digital Connection**: Thanks to social media, messaging apps, and video conversations, getting in touch with faraway friends and family members is now simpler than ever in the digital age. Strive to stay in touch and keep these relationships going.

10. **Community Service**: Taking part in service initiatives can help you meet people who share your dedication to changing the world in addition to having a good impact on your community. A strong sense of connection and belonging to the community may result from this.

You can improve your general emotional and psychological well-being, strengthen your relationships with others, and increase your social participation by incorporating these techniques into your daily life.

Understanding how Healthy Relationships can Support Cortisol Regulation and Energy Restoration

The following are some ways that healthy relationships might improve cortisol management and energy restoration.

Cortisol Management:

1. **Reduces Stress:** Relationships with reassuring relatives, friends, or partners can serve as a stress reducer. A person with social support may find that potentially stressful situations seem less dangerous, which may reduce their body's reaction to stress, including their release of cortisol.

2. **Sense of Safety and Security:** Feelings of safety and security can be strengthened by positive interactions. People's bodies tend to trigger the parasympathetic nervous system, which balances the sympathetic nervous system's activation brought on by stress, when they feel supported. This change can encourage healing and relaxation while lowering cortisol production.

3. **Positive Social Interactions:** The hormone oxytocin, which is linked to stress relief and bonding, can be elevated by participating in positive social interactions. By neutralizing the effects of cortisol, oxytocin helps lower stress levels and promote a more balanced and well-regulated stress response system.

Energy Restoration:

1. **Emotional Support**: Positive emotional support from wholesome connections can lift one's spirits and lessen depressing and anxious feelings, which frequently sap one's vitality. People who have access to emotional resources are better able to handle stress and recover from its draining effects more quickly.

2. **Better Sleep Quality**: An important part of energy regeneration is getting better sleep, which can be facilitated by the emotional stability that comes from having strong connections. Increased cortisol levels are linked to poor sleep, which can lead to a vicious cycle of stress and exhaustion. By encouraging calmness and lowering anxiety before bed, supportive relationships can aid in interrupting this pattern.

3. **Shared Activities**: Engaging in fun activities with close friends and family helps restore energy and offer a healing respite from stress. Positive experiences like this can improve general wellbeing and help people become more resilient to stress.

CHAPTER SEVEN

EXPLORING THE GUT-BRAIN CONNECTION

T HE ENTERIC NERVOUS SYSTEM (ENS) of the gastrointestinal tract and the central nervous system (CNS), which consists of the brain and spinal cord, are connected by a fascinating and intricate bidirectional communication system known as the "gut-brain connection." This link encompasses a variety of physiological, psychological, and emotional interactions and demonstrates the substantial impact that gut health has on mental well-being and vice versa.

Understanding the Bidirectional Communication between the Gut and the Brain via the Vagus Nerve

The gut-brain axis, which refers to the bidirectional communication between the gut and the brain, is a multidimensional and complex network that is essential to general health and well-being. The neurological system, immunological system, and endocrine (hormonal) pathways are some of the direct and indirect channels involved in this communication pathway. A crucial direct channel for messages traveling from the gut to the brain is the vagus nerve. The vagus nerve, which is a component of the gut-brain axis, allows for two-way communication between the brain and the gut. Gut-to-brain signals can impact emotional and cognitive regions of the brain, influencing emotions, stress levels, and feelings of hunger and fullness. For example:

1. **Microbiota-Generated Signals:** The trillions of microorganisms that make up the gut microbiota can produce metabolites and other

compounds, like bacterial peptides, tryptophan metabolites, and short-chain fatty acids, that can act on the vagus nerve or circulatory pathways to influence brain function. Additionally essential to the growth and operation of the immune system is the gut microbiota. Signals from active immune cells in the gut can reach the brain and affect behavior and neuroinflammation there.

2. **Hormonal Signals:** The brain can be signaled to regulate hunger, fullness, and digestion processes by the many hormones secreted by the gut in response to food intake and digestion. One important channel for these hormone signals is the vagus nerve. On the other hand, the brain can regulate a variety of gastrointestinal activities, including motility, secretion, and immunological responses. As an illustration:

3. **Stress Reaction:** Through the hypothalamic-pituitary-adrenal (HPA) axis, the brain's reaction to stress can affect gut function and microbiota composition. The vagus nerve modulates the effects of stress on the gut.

4. **Appetite and Digestion:** Through the vagus nerve, the brain may influence gut activities like blood flow, motility, and enzyme release to help with digestion and nutrition absorption.

Introducing Techniques To Support Gut Health And Optimize Vagal Tone

Maintaining general well-being requires supporting gut health and managing vagal tone because of their important roles in the autonomic nervous system balance and the gut-brain link. The following methods and way of living adjustments can assist in reaching these objectives:

1. Eating a diverse range of plant-based foods gives you the fiber your gut bacteria needs to thrive. Incorporate whole grains, legumes, fruits, and veggies into your diet.

2. Include foods high in beneficial bacteria, such as yogurt, kefir, sauerkraut, and kimchi, in your diet. These beneficial bacteria are fed by prebiotic foods including asparagus, bananas, garlic, and onions.

3. Maintaining digestive health, encouraging nutrient absorption, and avoiding constipation all depend on drinking adequate water.

4. Limit Sugar and Processed meals: An excessive amount of sugar and processed meals can upset the balance of the microbiome, preferring dangerous bacteria over helpful ones.

5. Chew everything properly and slowly to help with digestion and nutrient absorption, which lowers the risk of gastrointestinal distress.

Exploring the Impact of Gut Health on Cortisol Regulation and Overall Energy Levels

Microbiome Metabolites: Short-chain fatty acids (SCFAs), which are produced by the gut microbiota, have been shown to have an impact on behavior and brain function. Through the vagus nerve, these compounds can send signals to the brain that affect mood, stress response, and cognitive abilities.

Immune System Activation: In reaction to inflammation or illness, the brain can receive signals from the gut immune system. The brain's functioning can be impacted by cytokines and other inflammatory markers, which may result in behavioral and emotional abnormalities. These immunological signals can be transmitted from the vagus nerve to the brain, concentrating on the vagus nerve's role in the gut-brain-immune axis.

Hormonal Signals: The stomach secretes ghrelin and leptin, two hormones that regulate appetite and have an impact on mood and cognitive abilities. Through the vagus nerve or directly through the bloodstream, these hormones can communicate with the brain.

How The Brain And Gut Communicate To Influence Digestive Functions:

1. **Digestive Processes:** Through the vagus nerve, the brain can send signals to the gut that either stimulate or inhibit the production of enzymes, gastric acid secretion, and gut motility. This control makes sure

that digestion meets the needs of the body, particularly when it comes to relaxation or stress.

2. **Stress Response:** Through the vagus nerve, the brain's response to stress can directly impact the gut, changing factors such as gut motility, permeability, and even the makeup of the microbiome.

CHAPTER EIGHT

THE POWER OF SELF-COMPASSION AND EMOTIONAL REGULATION

IMAGINE YOUR MIND TO BE A GARDEN, WITH your thoughts serving as seeds to be planted. Self-compassion and emotional regulation are like the sunlight and water that sustain this garden. Without self-compassion, the garden may become parched and neglected, with weeds of self-criticism and doubt taking root. Emotional regulation, like pruning and weeding, helps control which thoughts thrive and which is eliminated. Just as a gardener employs tools to nurture the soil and promote healthy plant development, self-compassion softens our mental soil, making it more susceptible to positive, caring thoughts. This care enables flowers of resilience, calm, and joy to bloom abundantly. With consistent attention and kindness to oneself, the garden of the mind becomes a robust and flourishing area, regardless of the external situations. This well maintained garden not only lives, but thrives, demonstrating the transforming potential of self-compassion and emotional regulation in producing a healthy mental environment.

Understanding the Role of Self-Compassion in Vagal Tone Regulation

Being compassionate, understanding, and forgiving to oneself is central to the idea of self-compassion, especially in the face of hardship or failure. This method of regulating emotions and self-awareness can have a significant effect on vagal tone, emphasizing the complex relationship between mental and physical states. Self-compassion, for example, fosters positive emotional states that can increase vagal tone, which in turn can improve both mental and physical health. An outline of the role of self-compassion regulating vagal tone is provided below:

1. **Heart rate variability -** It has been found that practicing self-compassion increases HRV. A high heart rate variability (HRV) is indicative of a robust and adaptable cardiovascular system that can effectively handle stress and revert to a relaxed state more rapidly.

2. **Reducing Psychological Stress** - Psychological stress is linked to decreased activation of the sympathetic nervous system (fight or flight response) and increased activation of the parasympathetic nervous system (rest and digest), which is facilitated by the vagus nerve.

3. **Promoting Emotional Health** - Self-compassion promotes a happy emotional state and lessens unpleasant emotions that might interfere with vagal tone, such as anxiety and depression. Increased vagal activity, which improves physiological flexibility and resilience, is associated with positive feelings.

4. **Promoting Social Connection** - Feelings of loneliness can be diminished by strengthening social ties and acknowledging our shared humanity through self-compassion. Research indicates that engaging in positive social interactions might enhance vagal tone, hence augmenting emotional and physical well-being.

Exploring how Self-Compassion Practices can Influence Cortisol Levels and Energy Restoration

Self-compassion techniques, such as being kind, understandings, and accepting of oneself when facing challenges, have a big effect on physiological reactions, especially cortisol levels and energy recovery. Self-compassion exercises can be a very effective way to reduce the negative effects of stress, strengthen psychological resilience, and improve physical health. A look at some of the ways in which self-compassion exercises can affect cortisol levels and aid in energy restoration is provided below:

1. **Reduction of Stress Response:** Engaging in self-compassionate activities can help people feel less stressed, which in turn reduces the body's need to release cortisol. A more balanced cortisol response can result from people responding to stress with less negative feelings and thoughts when they take on a more sympathetic and nonjudgmental attitude toward themselves.

2. **Emotional Regulation**: Self-compassion promotes emotional regulation, enabling people to feel and deal with unpleasant feelings in a more healthy way. The hypothalamic-pituitary-adrenal (HPA) axis, which regulates cortisol secretion, may not become overactive due to this enhanced emotional regulation, which would lessen the overall stress response.

3. **Better Sleep:** Excessive cortisol levels, particularly at night, can interfere with sleep cycles and make it difficult to get a good night's sleep. Self-

compassion techniques can result in higher sleep quality, which is crucial for energy restoration and general health, by lowering stress and fostering emotional well-being.

4. **Enhanced healing:** Self-compassion activities can promote physical healing by inducing a relaxation response. The body may concentrate more on healing functions, like tissue repair and energy replenishment, when it is not under stress, which enhances vitality and overall wellbeing.

5. **Enhanced Psychological Resilience**: Self-compassion encourages psychological resilience, which can result in better coping mechanisms when faced with stress. This resilience can keep mental and physical energy stores from running low, allowing people to stay more energetic even in trying circumstances.

CHAPTER NINE

CREATING A VAGAL RESET ROUTINE

BY ACTIVATING AND STIMULATING THE VAGUS NERVE, which is essential for controlling your body's relaxation response, a vagal reset routine can drastically improve your well-being. The parasympathetic nervous system, also known as the "rest and digest" system, includes the vagus nerve. In addition to fostering a sense of peace and wellbeing, stimulating this nerve can help lower stress, anxiety, and inflammation.

Integrating Breathwork, Movement, Mindfulness, And Social Engagement Into A Daily Routine

A holistic approach to well-being can be created by integrating social engagement, movement, breathwork, and mindfulness into your daily routine. This will balance your mental and physical health. This integrated habit can help you feel more connected and like you belong, as well as increase your ability to handle stress and regulate your emotions. Here's how to apply these routines in your day-to-day life:

Morning: Move and practice mindfulness first

1. **Early-morning meditation**: Start your day by focusing on the present moment for five to ten minutes with mindfulness meditation. To start your day off on a positive note, pay attention to your breath or engage in a loving-kindness meditation.

2. **Movement Exercise**: Take a quick stroll or participate in a light movement exercise like yoga or tai chi. This promotes a peaceful and well-balanced start to your day by assisting with bodily awakening, circulation improvement, and vagal tone stimulation.

Midday: Mindfulness and Breath exercises

1. **Before lunch, schedule a five-minute breathwork session:** Stress can be decreased and focus improved with methods like box breathing and the 4-7-8 approach. Resetting your physiological state with breathwork can also help you relax and lower your cortisol levels.
2. **Mindfulness Breaks**: Throughout your workday, take quick pauses to practice mindfulness. This might be as easy as eating mindfully over lunch and paying close attention to the flavors and textures of your food, or it can be as easy as pausing between jobs to intentionally relax your body and take deep breaths.

Evening: Reflective Movement and Social Involvement

1. **Social Connection:** Schedule time for mingling with others. This could be going to a community event, video chatting with a buddy, or having supper with the family. Positive social interactions can stimulate the social engagement system, improving emotions of support and connection.

2. **Reflective Movement:** Take part in a reflective movement exercise in the evening, such as a quick jog or a mild yoga flow. Take this time to think back on the day, paying particular attention to how your body moves and how you are feeling. This can help you unwind and calm down from the day's activities.

Before going to sleep: Relax by practicing mindfulness.

1. **Gratitude Journaling:** Take a few minutes to jot down your blessings for the day. Gratitude can help you focus on the good things in your life rather than the stresses in it, which will improve your mental health.

2. **Mindfulness Meditation:** To assist relax and get ready for sleep, close your day with a mindfulness meditation. Techniques that emphasize body scanning or breathe awareness are very useful for lulling oneself into a peaceful sleep.

Developing Personalized Somatic Practices to Support Vagal Tone Regulation and Cortisol Balance

Personalized somatic practices can help support the modulation of vagal tone and achieve a balance in cortisol levels, which can enhance resilience and general well-being. Somatic practices emphasize movement, consciousness, and breathing as key components in fostering health, with a focus on the body's internal experience and the mind-body connection.

Here's how to create a customized routine that uses somatic techniques to achieve the ideal level of physiological balance:

1. **Determine Stress Levels:** Start by evaluating your present stress levels and the physical signs of those levels. Recognizing the physical manifestations of stress, such as tense muscles and shallow breathing, might assist you in modifying your techniques to target these regions.

2. **Determine Your Preferences:** Think about the movement and mindfulness techniques that you find most uplifting. While some people find peace in careful, patient motions like Tai Chi, others might enjoy more dynamic exercises like dancing.

Create Your Morning Routine: Turn On and Turn Off

Start with mild stretching or postures from yoga that help arouse the body. In order to stimulate the vagus nerve and encourage a relaxed, parasympathetic state, concentrate on deep, diaphragmatic breathing. Incorporate a mindful breathing method that corresponds to your level of energy in the morning. The body's energy can be balanced with methods like alternate nostril breathing, and morning worry and stress can be minimized with a few minutes of box breathing.

Midday: Focus

1. **Dynamic Movement:** To improve mood and energy levels, incorporate a physical activity that speeds up heart rate and uses the entire body, such as a vigorous walk. This can help regulate cortisol levels, especially when done outside in the sun.

2. **Focused Relaxation:** Set aside some time for focused relaxation techniques, such as body scan meditation or progressive muscle relaxation. This can aid in easing tense muscles and restoring normal cortisol levels over the day.

Evening: Unwind

1. **Reflective Movement:** To assist the down regulation of the nervous system, practice reflective movement in the evenings. One such practice is Qigong, which blends moderate movement, breathing, and meditation.

2. **Relaxation through Breathwork:** Utilize breathwork methods like the 4-7-8 technique or deep abdominal breathing to improve vagal tone and support cortisol balance. These methods are intended to help people relax and get ready for bed.

Understanding the Importance of Consistency and Self-Care in Maintaining Optimal Energy Levels

Various aspects, such as stress management, food, exercise, sleep patterns, and emotional health, might affect one's energy levels. Maintaining a regular schedule of self-care can assist control these variables, which can enhance general health and energy levels. The following explains the importance of self-care and consistency:

1. **Consistency**: Practicing self-care on a regular basis facilitates the development of habits that eventually become automatic. Making healthy decisions on a daily basis becomes less of a mental strain as a result of becoming consistent in your routine.

2. **Biological Clock Regulation:** Your body's internal clocks, or circadian rhythms, are regulated by maintaining regular sleep and eating routines. This can raise energy levels all day long and enhance the quality of sleep.

3. **Gains over Time:** Exercise and eating a balanced diet are two examples of self-care behaviors that have gained over time. To reap these benefits, such as; boosted mood, improved metabolism, increased stamina, and consistency over time, it is essential.

4. **Physical Health:** Basic self-care habits that have a direct impact on energy levels include regular physical activity, a balanced diet, enough hydration, and enough sleep. They help the body function at its best by supporting its physiological needs.

5. **Emotional Well-Being**: By partaking in activities that promote mental health and relaxation, such as mindfulness exercises, social activities, and hobbies, one can avoid burnout and minimize stress. This keeps the energy levels from dropping by preventing emotional exhaustion.

CHAPTER TEN

THRIVING WITH RENEWED ENERGY AND VITALITY

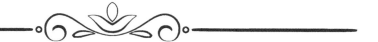

A COMPLETE STRATEGY THAT ADDRESSES mental and emotional stability as well as lifestyle modifications are necessary to thrive with restored vigor and energy. It involves taking care of your body, mind, and soul in ways that support and elevate you. The journey of cortisol control and vagal reset is a thorough investigation of the complex interactions between our bodies and thoughts, emphasizing the importance of mindfulness and self-care in preserving our wellbeing. Here's a summary of the main ideas and lessons this adventure taught me: Throughout this trip, the vagus nerve emerges as a key player, controlling our physiological condition and serving as the primary pathway of the parasympathetic nervous system. Vagal tone can be greatly increased by practicing deep breathing, mindfulness meditation, gentle yoga, and other techniques that activate the vagus nerve. This increases resilience to stress and promotes a sense of calm.

The stress hormone, cortisol, is essential to our body's stress response. Chronically high cortisol levels can be harmful, even though they are necessary for survival. Consistently practicing mindfulness, breathing exercises, physical exercise, and social interaction creates an atmosphere that is conducive to the growth and well-being of individuals. Our bodies and minds both benefit from practices that increase relaxation and stress resilience, which raises our quality of life overall. Maintaining ideal energy levels and well-being requires paying attention to our bodies, acknowledging our limitations, and showing ourselves compassion and understanding. This trip is about developing a compassionate and aware approach to our everyday lives, not only about reaching our destination.

Celebrating the Journey

The process of raising vagal tone is evidence of the influence that lifestyle decisions and self-care routines have on our well-being. It emphasizes how crucial it is for us to lead mindful lives and engage in physical activity, social interaction, and healthy eating. While we rejoice in these advantages, we also recognize that health is a holistic concept and that our physical, mental, and emotional well-being are intricately linked.

This celebration takes into account the wider consequences for the health of the community and society as a whole, in addition to the individual advantages. It is possible to create a society that is more robust, caring, and connected by promoting behaviors that increase vagal tone. We contribute to a culture of wellness that appreciates and promotes overall vitality and well-being as we investigate and adopt these practices further.

Empowering Readers to Continue Prioritizing Somatic Practices For Sustained Energy And Resilience

One of the most important things you can do to maintain your energy, resilience, and general well-being is to give somatic activities priority. Somatic practices offer a comprehensive approach to wellbeing that unifies the mind, body, and spirit. They stress the body's involvement in psychological health. By engaging in these routines, we improve not just our physical health but also our mental and emotional toughness. The following are methods to enable you and other people to carry on incorporating somatic practices into everyday life for sustained advantages:

Set Realistic Expectation

1. **Start Little:** Start with brief, doable workouts that you can fit into your calendar with ease. Breathwork or light movement, even for a short while, can yield big results.

2. **Be Specific:** Decide on specific goals instead of different ones, eg; "do more yoga," like "attend a yoga class twice a week" or "practice 10 minutes of mindful breathing every morning."

Create a Routine

1. **The Secret Is Consistency**: To create consistency, try incorporating somatic techniques into your everyday routine. This may be a yoga practice in the evening, a walk in the afternoon, or a meditation in the morning.

Explore and Experiment

1. Search for different somatic techniques, including Tai Chi, Yoga, Feldenkrais, and dance therapy. Finding what speaks to you can help

you maintain the practice's interest and enjoyment. Take classes or workshops to pick up new skills and viewpoints. Participating in a community can provide inspiration and support.

Adopt Mindfulness

1. Include awareness in routine tasks, such as walking or mindful eating. This might support you throughout the day to remain grounded and in the moment.
2. To center yourself and instantly handle stress, regularly focus on your breath, which is a basic somatic technique.

Educate and Analyze

1. Learn about the theory and science underlying somatic techniques. Gaining an understanding of their advantages might increase your dedication and drive.

Create a Supportive Community

1. **Share Your Own Experience:** Make connections with people who have a somatic practice interest. You and your peers can both benefit from and be inspired by sharing your struggles and accomplishments.

2. **Group Practice:** Take part in somatic practices with friends, family, or local groups whenever you can. The group energy has the power to elevate the encounter and promote a feeling of unity.

CONCLUSION

EMBRACING THE VAGAL RESET LIFESTYLE

I T'S IMPORTANT TO STRIKE A BALANCE AND incorporate these routines into your lifestyle in a way that feels fun and sustainable in order to promote vagal health. Making deliberate decisions that improve your well-being is more important than striving for perfection. Make a small initial alteration or two, then work your way up to more. Observe your body and make any necessary adjustments. Adopting the vagal reset lifestyle is a path to increased resilience, happiness, and health. You can start by doing the following:

1. Practice mindful breathing

2. Move your body more often, it doesn't have to be 'exercise'

3. Build healthy relationships

4. Practice mindfulness

5. Eat a diet high in fiber, foods that reduce inflammation, and probiotics

6. Participate in activities that make you happy

7. Digital balance

Summarizing Key Insights And Takeaways From The Book

Taking up a vagal reset lifestyle, as described in the thorough investigation of techniques meant to improve wellbeing by activating the vagus nerve and controlling cortisol levels, has several advantages for mental and physical health.

The following are the book's main conclusions and insights:

1. **The Vagus Nerve:** Recognizing the vagus nerve as an essential part of the parasympathetic nervous system allows us to appreciate its profound impact on our body's ability to respond to stress, control our emotions, and maintain homeostasis in general. Calm, resiliency, and wellbeing can result from stimulating the vagus nerve in different ways.

2. **Practical Techniques for Vagal Stimulation**: The book offers a number of simple methods for stimulating the vagus nerve, such as mindful breathing exercises, cold exposure, and physical activities that promote relaxation and stress reduction.

3. **Importance of Social Connections:** Establishing and maintaining healthy relationships is essential for stimulating the vagus nerve's social engagement component, highlighting the significance of support networks and a sense of community in our lives. The relationship between mindfulness and emotional well-being is well-established. Regular mindfulness exercises and meditation improve vagal tone, which in turn improves emotional regulation and stress tolerance.

4. **Diet and Gut Health:** A diet strong in fiber, probiotics, and anti-inflammatory foods is crucial for preserving a balanced stress response and general wellbeing. This is particularly true given the connection between the gut-brain axis and the vagus nerve.

5. **Good Emotional Experiences**: Gratitude, joy, and laughing are examples of activities that have a favorable effect on vagal tone, demonstrating the significant influence that happy emotions have on our health.

6. **The Importance of Restorative Sleep**: Quality sleep is essential for regulating the body's stress response systems, particularly the vagus nerve, highlighting the importance of a relaxing and consistent bedtime routine.

7. **The Health Benefits of Laughing and Singing**: The vagus nerve can be stimulated by simple actions like laughing, singing, and even gargling. This illustrates the variety of ways in which this important nerve can be activated in daily life.

8. **The Need for Digital Balance:** Being mindful about your screen time, particularly before bed, will improve sleep quality and reduce stress, which will enhance vagal health and general wellness.

9. **The Path to Better Health**: Adopting a vagal reset lifestyle is a deliberate decision-making process to improve overall health. Finding balance and progressively implementing enjoyable and sustainable habits that promote vagal health are key.

Encouraging Readers to Embrace a Lifestyle Centered Around Vagal Tone Regulation and Cortisol Balance

Adopting a lifestyle focused on cortisol balance and vagal tone management is a holistic approach that has a substantial impact on your emotional well-being, stress resilience, and general quality of life. It goes beyond improving your physical health. By concentrating on exercises that uplift your vagus nerve and keep your cortisol levels in check, you're making an investment in a wellness base that will see you through all of life's ups and downs. To assist you in starting this fulfilling journey, consider the following inspiring tips:

Recognize first how important vagal tone and cortisol levels are to your overall health. Better stress management, deeper relaxation, better digestion, and a stronger immune system can all be brought about by a balanced cortisol level and a well-regulated vagus nerve. You may be inspired to prioritize these elements of your health if you are aware of their benefits.

Start modest and doable, such as adding a few minutes of deep breathing exercises to your daily routine, introducing cold showers gradually, or setting aside time for mindfulness exercises. Over time, these little adjustments can add up to big advantages. Enjoy the rituals you decide to adopt into your daily life. Laughter, singing, social interaction, or experimenting with new forms of movement such as dancing, tai chi, or yoga are some ways to express yourself. These tasks turn from being chores to treasured parts of your daily routine when you like doing them.

Talk about your journey with loved ones, close friends, or a network of support. Participating in social activities gives you incentive and accountability in addition to stimulating your vagus nerve. It's possible that others might like to accompany you, in which case you may create a shared experience that strengthens bonds and improves the trip. Always look for resources and information regarding cortisol balance and vagal tone regulation. You'll be in a better position to make wise choices regarding your health and wellbeing the more you comprehend about the research underlying these routines and their advantages.

Observe how your body and mind react to various exercises. It's vital to pay attention to your personal experiences and modify your strategy based on what you find to be effective. Appreciate your accomplishments and practice self-compassion when things don't go according to plan. Periodically review your trip and acknowledge the shifts in your overall state of well-being. You can recognize the strides you've made and pinpoint areas in which you still have room for improvement by keeping a journal or talking to others about your experiences.

Inspiring Continued Exploration and Growth In The Journey Toward Optimal Health And Vitality

Setting off on a path toward maximum health and vitality is a continuous process that calls for a strong sense of self-discovery, curiosity, and resilience. This is a journey characterized by ongoing learning, trying new things, and developing. Here are some tips to help you stay motivated and interested while you travel through this:

Adopt a growth mentality as you embark on your health journey — the conviction that you can become well with commitment and effort. This way of looking at things promotes resilience, assists in embracing difficulties, and turns roadblocks into chances for growth and learning. Make your trip fun by establishing attainable, dynamic goals. Celebrate your accomplishments when you reach each milestone and then establish new objectives that push you to reach farther. This never-ending cycle of creating goals and achieving them drives advancement and motivation.

Be willing to investigate new methods and fields of study that can improve your health. Every new experience you have can enrich your health journey, whether it's learning about other nutritional philosophies, trying out new workout routines, or practicing different mindfulness practices. Keep learning new things about wellness and health. Take workshops, read books, listen to podcasts, and follow industry experts. This gives you constant inspiration in addition to keeping you updated on the newest findings and fashions.

Embrace the company of like-minded people who are as passionate about health and vitality as you are. Connecting with others offers support, encouragement, and a sense of community. This can be achieved through attending health and wellness events, joining a local workout group, or engaging in online forums. Take regular breaks to consider your route.

Evaluate what is and isn't working and be prepared to modify your strategy as necessary. By reflecting, you can take stock of your accomplishments, draw lessons from your past, and decide on the best course of action. You will undoubtedly face obstacles and setbacks on this road. During these times, treat yourself with compassion and understanding, just as you would a close friend. Resilience is fostered by self-compassion, which makes it simpler to recover and carry on further.

Finally, enjoy the trip rather than focusing only on the end point. Savor the moments of discovery, rejoice in the little things, and take pleasure in the pursuits that enhance your wellbeing. Long-term engagement and commitment are more likely to be maintained during a pleasurable journey.

Made in the USA
Las Vegas, NV
10 May 2024